Antonio Raimondi
Rocco Raimondi

Sylvester Stallone:

Never Give Up

All rights reserved.
No part of this publication may be reproduced, stored in a retrieval system, or transmitted, in any form or by any means, electronic, mechanical, photocopying, recording or otherwise, without the prior permission of the publishers.

Antonio Raimondi

Rocco Raimondi

"Sylvester Stallone: Never Give Up"

ISBN   9798692233929

Italy, 2020

We grew up with his films full of values and valuable teachings.

Dedicated to the Man and Actor who most inspired us in life.

To Sylvester Stallone.

INDEX

7	**PROLOGUE**
14	**ROCKY: A TIMELESS SUCCESS**
22	*TO WIN*
25	*BELIEVE IN YOURSELF*
31	*LOYALTY AND FRIENDSHIP*
39	*TO START FROM SCRATCH*
48	*GET INVOLVED*
54	**LOCK UP**
62	**RAMBO: A MAN MARKED BY WAR**
76	*RAMBO: FIRST BLOOD PART II*
88	*RAMBO III*
95	*RAMBO*
103	*RAMBO: LAST BLOOD*
111	**OVER THE TOP**
119	AUDIOVISUAL SOURCES

"When there is a problem with people who I thought were friends, they say: "It's business!".". But for me it's not like that, it's not just business. When you are friends with someone, business inevitably becomes secondary.

I'm a loyal guy and friendship is everything to me, so sometimes I get screwed.

When you always act from your heart, you end up hurting yourself: it's normal, but at least you've been true to yourself. This is what really matters.

For twenty years I was very ambitious, I tried to do everything and I got caught up in the mania of doing as many things as possible, of obtaining every possible advantage: power, fame, notoriety. In this environment this is how things go, there is little to do and to live like this you have to give up private life. I did it too and looking back now I can say that it was not worth it, I didn't know it then: I was raised with that concept.

Ours was not exactly an easy life at the beginning, that of our family can be considered a true American story.

Our parents were typical Americans of those years but they came from completely different contexts. My brother and I ended up in military school.

Having grown up in that way pushed us to take refuge in fantasy because reality was not at all as it should have been.

Sly was very skinny as a child and had slight paralysis on his face, so they all teased him and calling himself Sylvester didn't help.

It was the golden age of American superhero comics (there was Flash, there was Marvel comics).

What struck me most was Hercules: I took him as a model of life, I told myself that I wanted to become like him, that was the body I would have when I grew up and look that I was really very, very thin. I got completely caught up in it, I mean I hurt myself trying to do the same things Superman did on TV (he jumped off a building and I thought I could jump off the roof, dressed in a barber's cape and a couple of boots).

He broke every bone he had, but he didn't give up and started lifting weights, he started working out. We had weights all over the place.

Even though I knew that I would never get to Steve Reeves' levels, I decided to follow that path (I became his friend and he was a role model for me, which I still try to reach today).

He was told he could never do it. They said: you have a crooked mouth, you don't understand what you are saying and you are too muscular, you don't have the right look. When everyone talks to you like that it is inevitable that the Rocky spirit will come out: Rocky just wants to have a chance (like all of us, at least we want to try). At that time we shared the apartment.

It was either very hot or freezing cold and full of cockroaches. It was awful. It cost $ 71 a month and was right above a subway stop, so after 81 years of shaking it was all unsafe.

He slept on the bed and I on the floor, the next night we swapped. We had only one room without a bathroom which was in the corridor. We put food on the windowsill to keep it cold because we didn't have a fridge. We walked the streets of New York as if there were only us (in sweatpants), no one was walking around in tracksuits then. And we had Converse shoes (Adidas weren't famous yet). And we had some t-shirts that I will never forget, they were super tight (we took them one size smaller to make them look more macho). We would go around Manatthan and people would turn to look at us and we weren't big at all but we thought we were. We had biceps in sight and long hair, we went dressed like this even when we didn't go to the gym, just to let people watch us.

It was fun, we went around like that. And those were important years: the years in which I built my philosophy of life.

Career before Rocky wasn't easy at all, I couldn't work because I wasn't physically suitable. I was not born with a beautiful appearance or with a super body.

I had to sweat to earn everything.

In the first three or four films (minor roles) I was always playing the bad guy but I didn't feel like that at all. I looked in the mirror and saw something completely different from how others looked at me. I saw a cool guy, even a charming one, but the others saw a robber, a thug, one of those who chase people. The first impression is the fundamental, so you are doomed to always play the same role until you prove that you are different. **If I really wanted to be understood, if I really wanted to do something that followed my philosophy of life, I would have to make something happen because the opportunity would never have come by itself. I should have done it all by myself.** I isolated myself from the world, tried to eliminate all distractions, even went so far as to darken the windows by painting them black.

I had to choose whether to continue having fun, going to parties and doing what you normally do as a kid or devote myself to something more serious. So it was a self-imposed exile, writing is a process, something very noble that can give you incredible strength. Like when you try to find the right phrase for sixteen hours in a row, when you finally succeed it is an enlightenment (you can jump from your chair in excitement but these are rare moments!).

I had just auditioned for a small part and as I left the room I had an idea, I said "If you are interested I'll write" and they replied: "Sure, if you have something come back", if I hadn't had that idea and if they didn't had said "come back" maybe I would never have become what I am now.

I started writing like crazy, for ninety percent it wasn't that great but the idea and the right spirit was already in those pages (referring to Rocky's script). When they read it, they said they liked the story and they would buy it but I wouldn't have to go into it, so I made some calculations and selling Rocky would make maybe fifteen thousand dollars, it would be over soon, then I would regret for the rest of my life because the movie talked just about this: **Never give up.** And so I asked them to at least allow me to try and when they refused I said: "Then no, it doesn't matter." It's amazing what can be achieved by saying no.

Only thanks to the blessed ignorance of the youth did I continue to say no and to stay on my positions until I got the part temporarily (at the first mistake I would have been discarded). So I was sure we would do a week of filming and then they would kick me out and do it all over again.

Now everyone denies it, but I'm sure it would have happened like this. It was in the air, but luckily John Avildsen and the production decided to shoot the dramatic scenes first.

The first scene we did was the one in which I am a thug (I run after a customer on the riverside, I hit him against the wall and I say: "You owe me money. If you want to dance you have to pay the orchestra!").

After the scene they said to each other: "Hey, maybe there really is something good here". Thank God we shot that scene first.

The subject was quite obscure for the film canons of the time. There was no romance, there was no comedy, he was a boxer, or rather an ex-boxer to whom everything went wrong.

When they told me it was a boxing movie, I said no. It was actually a love movie about Adriana (Talia Shire) and the guy who was trying to go out with her.

I thought I couldn't make it, that I was out of my league, that I got into trouble. **Without Adriana there is no music in the film, there is nothing».**

(*Sylvester Stallone and his brother Frank in italics*).

Before becoming rich and famous, Sylvester Stallone was having a really bad time to the point that he had to sell his trusty dog named Butkus for about forty dollars, which he will be able to buy later for fifteen thousand dollars from the new owner. Sylvester Stallone, in this regard, says: "It was worth every single penny spent.

Butkus was my best friend, my confidant, he always laughed at my jokes and cheered me up, he was the only living being who loved me for who I really was. Without him I wouldn't have had the strength to write Rocky scripts. He is still the background of my computer".

The turtles, present in the Rocky saga and bought right at the shop where Adriana works, to which they are shown in their meetings, are instead called Cuff and Link.

ROCKY
A timeless success

Often the most beautiful works of art arise from situations of suffering and discomfort.

This is certainly also the secret of the charm of the Rocky boxer.

Made in 1976 in less than a month on a low budget, it will win three Oscars and become an unprecedented success.

Six are the films of the well-known film saga: *Rocky, Rocky II, Rocky III, Rocky IV, Rocky V and Rocky Balboa.*

Rocky is the story of a timeless legend.

It all begins in the suburbs of Philadelphia, where Rocky, who until then has never made it to the professional world of boxing, earns his living under the guidance of an Italian-American gangster. He is friends with Paulie (Burt Young), with whom he meets at the bar and works in a slaughterhouse. Paulie's sister is Adriana, with a decidedly shy character, she works in a pet shop and is constantly courted by Rocky. On Thanksgiving they decide to go ice skating together. Rocky takes Adriana home where he manages to win a kiss from her. It is the beginning of the engagement and the long love story that will be the backbone of the entire saga.

The reigning heavyweight champion Apollo Creed (Carl Weathers) - who arrived on the occasion of the bicentenary of the founding of the United States of America - will challenge a random boxer (because of the absence of the official challenger due to injury): the "Stallone Italiano", Rocky Balboa. The news goes around the city and this leads Mickey (Burgess Meredith), Rocky's old coach (the protagonist was in fact training in a small and dark gym in the neighborhood) to visit him at the home. Here he offers himself as a manager in order to train Rocky. A debate begins where Mickey explains his experience and the reasons that led him to be there while Rocky responds with facts and justifications concerning the help he should have received in the past.

So Mickey, aware of Rocky's refusal, comes out of the apartment door and from here begins a sort of outpouring of Rocky to the old coach.

ROCKY: Took you long enough to get here. Took 10 years to come to my house. You don't like my house? My house stink? That's right, it stinks! I din't ask no favors from you! Talk about your prime. What about my prime, Mick? At least you had a prime! I ain't had no prime. I ain't had nothing. Legs are going, everything is going. Nobody's giving me nothing. Guy comes up, offers me a fight. Big deal. Wanna fight the fight? Yeah, I'll fight the big fight. I'm gonna go fight that big fight and I'm gonna get that! I'm gonna get that! And you wanna be ringside and see? Do you? You wanna help me out? Do you wanna see me get my face kicked in? Legs ain't working, nothing's working. Think I'll go and fight the champ. Yeah, I'll fight him. Get my face kicked in. And you come around here. You wanna move in with me? Come on in. It's a nice house! Real nice! Come on in! It stinks! This whole place stinks. You wanna help me out? Well, help me out! Come on. Help me out. I'm standing here! (*Rocky*, 1976).

Mickey is coming down the stairs of Rocky's house, he starts walking down the street but shortly after Rocky comes out running and goes to hug him under the poignant notes of Bill Conti: this is the beginning of the strong friendship that will bind them forever. Rocky is the reason for living that pushes Mickey to go on, to live again.

Each of us must have something in our existence to fight for, to keep going despite everything. This is the message in all Sylvester Stallone cult films.

This reason for living will be highlighted in a nostalgic montage in Rocky V, after the death of the old coach.

The relationship between Rocky and Mickey transcends the relational limits between athlete and manager, becoming paternal.

Mickey for Rocky is a true teacher of life, a trusted advisor and symbolically a guardian angel. The city of Philadelphia is shown mostly at night or at the first light of dawn.

For example, when Rocky gets up early in the morning to go for a run, greyness and mediocrity dominate in a gloomy environment where ambitions and prospects are scarce. In the Rocky movie saga the boxer's workouts and also those of the rivals occupy an important space in the narrative: the morning run with consequent staircase (72 stone steps in front of the entrance to the Philadelphia Museum of Art) accentuated by the fist in the air is iconic, symbol of victory.

The workouts in the slaughterhouse where Paulie works are also highly representative (beef quarters replace the punching bag). The message is clear: use everything we have at our disposal, overcoming the obstacles of life to try to reach a goal.

Both in the workouts, in the slaughterhouse and in the morning run sequences, including the Rocky staircase, there is a notable dynamism thanks to the use of the steadycam (whose inventor Garrett Brown, present as a Philadelphia cameraman) used to great effect a tool that, due to the low budget made available for the making of the film, would never have been possible to use).

The character of Adriana is fundamental for Rocky who finds in her his conscience, his support: the woman who chose him when everyone thought him invisible, as well as his willpower and his lifeline in the darkest moments, such as only true love can offer.

The meeting between the two is immediately in perfect harmony, both Rocky and Adriana have in common the fact that they want to get out of their periphery, intended both as a physical and purely personal place. Before the big meeting he will find comfort in Adriana and confess the following words to her (from which different emotions emerge: from fear to hope).

ROCKY: I was nobody. But that don't matter either, you know? 'Cause I was thinkin', it really don't matter if I lose this fight. It really don't matter if this guy opens my head, either. 'Cause all I wanna do is go the distance. Nobody's ever gone the distance with Creed, and if I can go that distance, you see, and that bell rings and I'm still standin', I'm gonna know for the first time in my life, see, that I weren't just another bum from the neighborhood. (*Rocky*, 1976)

Rocky, thanks to Adriana's love and sport (initially a relief valve, then a professional occupation as well as a fundamental step in the ethical and moral growth of the boxer), finds his personal dimension.

Intense training under the wise guidance of old Mickey will not be enough to defeat Apollo Creed in the great match, but he will find great difficulty thanks to Rocky's incredible strength.

He falls to the ground in the 14th round, apparently lacking in strength, but manages to get up for the last round and still hold out. The final verdict awards the points win to defending champion Apollo Creed.

The American morality of the man who wins at all costs is overturned. After dramas, grueling workouts, sweat, tears, blood and emotions, Rocky loses the match of life, but figuratively he overcomes his uncertainties and changes his life for the better thanks to love.

In the famous final, Rocky tries to push oneself through the crowd and shouts the name of his beloved several times: "Adrianaaa".

She runs to embrace him with all her love, in a final full of emotions.

«TO WIN»

It is 1979, the year of *Rocky II*.

Thanks to the visibility obtained from the match with Apollo Creed, Rocky is now able to marry and build a family with Adriana, while Apollo, feeling humiliated by the match, asks for a rematch.

Thanks to the money obtained from the match and due to physical problems, Rocky initially manages to stay away from the ring but the call is too strong as well as the desire for revenge (without sport there is a sort of wearing down of the very essence of Rocky) so he decides to accept the rematch.

Despite Adriana's health problems, caused by the difficult birth, he is always supported by Mickey who helps him take victory in the last second of the last round after two knockouts.

«You're gonna eat lightning and you're gonna crap thunder».

(Mickey addressing Rocky. *Rocky II*, 1979)

The direction of *Rocky II* entrusted to Sylvester Stallone (while in the previous chapter to John G. Avildsen) is not affected by any slowness, as well as the pace of training and those of the fight between the two boxers.

The gloomy and greyish atmospheres of Philadelphia now appear warmer also in relation to the economic conditions of the protagonists that become clearer like their lives.

«BELIEVE IN YOURSELF»

In the third chapter of the saga dated 1982, Rocky, reigning heavyweight champion, savors well-being and luxury, forgetting his humble origins.

The old Mickey combines easy matches (not sold) to protect Rocky from the fury of boxer Clubber Lang (MR T), loaded with all the experience of the road, yet another challenger to the world title who manages to make the Italian Stallion accept the challenge.

On the day of the match, the challenger boxer causes a fight in the corridor before the stadium and Mickey suffers a heart attack.

Rocky would like to cancel the match but is encouraged by the manager who stays in the locker room with Adriana, getting worried and distracted in the ring.

MR T, in the 2nd round, beat Rocky with a crushing KO, securing the title of heavyweight champion.

Rocky, defeated and disappointed, he immediately returns to the locker room where he helplessly witnesses the death of dear Mickey.

```
ROCKY: Mick? Mick.
MICKEY: What? … What? … What? Is it
over?
ROCKY: Yeah, it's all over.
MICKEY: Hey, listen, what happened?
ROCKY: It was a knockout.
MICKEY: What round? What round?
ROCKY: Second round.
```

MICKEY: Yeah, I knew it. That's good. We did it, huh?
ROCKY: We did it. We did it.
MICKEY: All right.
ROCKY: You don't have to worry no more.
MICKEY: No. Good.
ROCKY: Everything's gonna be okay, Mick. You know?
MICKEY: I knew that we did it.
ROCKY: You gotta get to the hospital. You're not as young as you used to be.
MICKEY: You're the winner. We did everything right. I did everything...
ROCKY: No, no, listen. Wa ain't done everything right. Listen, we got more to do. Mick, whatever you want to do, we'll do it, okay?
MICKEY: I love you, kid. I love you.
ROCKY: Mick!
MICKEY: It hurts me.
ROCKY: Mick? Mick?! Mick... Don't go away, please, don't. We got more to do. We got more to do. We got... Oh, my God! Oh, Jesus... (*Rocky III,* 1982)

To alleviate Mickey's suffering, Rocky makes him believe he has won, thus giving him one last winner's joy before he dies. Among the most moving scenes of the entire saga.

In the Italian Stallone there is no longer any desire to fight: he is afflicted by the fear of the idea that he may have lost the trust of all those who believed in him and furthermore, the disappearance of his coach is the source of a moral defeat that throws into a darkness from which it seems almost impossible to get out.

Apollo Creed will help him overcome this depressive state, (who will visit the old gym where Rocky trained), who will propose himself as manager to prepare him for a rematch with MR T. Thanks to Apollo, his old coach Tony Evers (Tony Burton) also comes to the rescue: both initially try to train Rocky but without receiving any success.

Thus, Rocky is left alone, so that he can reflect and come back to believe in himself. Adriana manages to make the boxer find the determination hidden in the deepest depths of his soul.

The confrontation on the beach, where both Apollo and Adriana are present, is fundamental.

After an angry outburst from Rocky, Adriana reassures him with these words:

ADRIANA: Apollo thinks you can do it. So do I. You've got to want it for the right reasons… not for the guilt over Mickey, not the people, not for the title… not for money or me, but for you. Just you, just you alone.
ROCKY: And if I lose?
ADRIANA: Then you lose, but at least you lose with no excuses. No fear. I know you could live with that.
ROCKY: How'd you get so tough?
ADRIANA: I live with a fighter.
ROCKY: I really love you. I love you.
(*Rocky III*, 1982)

The scene ends with a kiss and a comforting hug. Now Rocky finally believes in himself again.

The race with Apollo on the beach with the final celebration will remain etched in Rocky's heart and will be the beginning of the hard training that will lead him to defeat MR T and recover the lost title.

«But the truth is, you didn't look hungry. Now when we fought... you had that eye of the tiger, man, the edge. You gotta get it back. The way to do that is to go to the beginning. You know what I mean? Maybe we could win it back together. Eye of the tiger, man!».
(Apollo addressing Rocky. *Rocky III*, 1982)

Tenacity and humility in a great and noble heart expressed by the *Eyes of the Tiger*, that is eyes full of adrenaline, of the desire to win, to resist until the end and to demonstrate one's abilities by overcoming all limits. Survivor's *Eye of The Tiger* is the soundtrack chosen and used to beautifully exalt all of this.

«LOYALTY AND FRIENDSHIP»

Fourth chapter of the saga: 1985. We are in the Reagan era and in the period of the Cold War between the United States of America and the Soviet Union, the clash between the ideals of American democracy and those of Communism.

This time the challenge to American boxing comes directly from the Soviet Union through an imposing Ivan Drago (Dolph Lundgren), Olympic medal holder.

Challenge rejected by Rocky but accepted by his friend Apollo, eager to return to fight since he has been away from the ring for about five years.

Trained by Rocky and Tony, Apollo now seems ready for the match.

Rocky tries to make him change his mind until the last and avoid the battle against the Soviet or at least postpone it for a few weeks: nothing to do. The match is enhanced in the broader context of American patriotism with plays of lights and costumes accompanied by the song *Living in America* by James Brown.

Ivan Drago's power is manifested immediately, Rocky insistently asks his friend to throw in the towel, but he proudly and repeatedly refuses until the last blow struck by the Russian that knocks him down, killing him. Apollo dies in the ring in Rocky's arms.

Death on his battlefield is symbolically the highest aspiration of a soldier who proudly gives his life to his homeland. He dies doing what he had always loved and for everything that kept him alive. Rocky, in addition to having to endure the death of his dear friend Apollo, ends up in the media storm for not having blocked the match before this tragedy occurred.

Apollo's death symbolizes the defeat of the United States of America with the Soviet Union. The rematch is a must.

Rocky, oppressed by a strong sense of guilt and revenge, decides to challenge Ivan Drago. The match, however, this time will take place on Russian soil on Christmas day without any cash prizes.

Adriana's words will not be enough to change Rocky's mind, whose determination is expressed in these words.

«No, maybe I can't win. Maybe the only thing I can do is just take everything he's got. But to beat me, he's gonna have to kill me. And to kill me, he's gonna have to have the heart to stand in front of me. And to do that, he's gotta be willing to die himself. I don't know if he's ready to do that. I don't know. I don't know». (Rocky addressing Adriana. *Rocky IV*, 1985)

Rocky gets into the car and begins to drive, memories of Apollo emerge in his mind, of the last tragic match and in general of all life experiences with people dear to him (a long and exciting flashback) under the notes of the specially chosen song: *No Easy Way Out* by Robert Tepper, whose refrain is as follows.

There's no easy way out

There's no hort cut home

There's no easy way out

Givin' in can't be wrong

Rocky leaves with his coach Tony and his friend Paulie, leaving Adriana and her son Robert at home, to whom, before leaving, he gives a real life lesson.

ROBERT: When will you be back?
ROCKY: Oh, pretty son.
ROBERT: Are you scared?
ROCKY: No.
ROBERT: Yes, you are. A little, maybe?
ROCKY: Well, wouldn't you be?
ROBERT: If a big giant man wanted to beat me up, I'd be real scared.

ROCKY: Well, the truth is, you know, sometimes... I do get a little scared. When I'm in that ring and I'm really getting hit on... and my arms hurt so much I can't even lift them... and I'm thinking: "I wish this guy would hit me on the chin... so I don't feel nothing anymore." Then there's another side that comes out that isn't so scared. There's another side that, like... wants to take more... that wants to go that one more round because by going that one more round when you don't think you can... It's what makes all the difference in your life. Do you now what I mean? I want you to remember one more thing. Remember that: Daddy thinks you're the best boy in the world. That Daddy loves you, no matter what. (*Rocky IV*, 1985)

«Taking another round when you think you can't make it is something that can change your whole life».

Under the rigorous attention of Soviet intelligence, Rocky arrives at his quarters (a farmhouse in the frozen Soviet steppe). Here, he immediately begins to train with all of himself. The training methods of Rocky and Ivan Drago are completely opposite: Rocky uses everything that nature offers while Ivan Drago is constantly followed by various specialized teams and is trained (and doped) with all the most sophisticated and innovative technological equipment. The lifting of weights in the barn near a burning fire, the races on the snow-capped mountains, the chopping wood until exhaustion, the lifting of the wagon inside which there are Adriana (who decides to join him to offer him closeness and courage) and Paulie, who are just part of the hard, wild and almost prehistoric training Rocky undergoes (all this is accompanied by John Cafferty's energetic *Hearts on Fire*). Match day arrives, followed on television by millions of Americans supporting Rocky from their Christmas-decorated homes. As happened to Ivan Drago in the American ring, Rocky is also booed continuously since his entrance.

Present and ready to watch the match is the entire Soviet Intelligencija (a Russian word indicating a social group representing the highest political, military, scientific and intellectual positions). Ivan Drago starts to put Rocky in trouble, who reacts in the second round and manages to injure his eyebrow. However, the Russian begins to get discouraged as the Italian stallion always gets up. The fight continues under the disbelief and embarrassment of the Soviet Intelligence and things inexorably really begin to change and the audience, also incredulous, begins to shout the name of Rocky loudly.

Rocky's prejudice towards Drago undergoes a change: from pure hatred towards his opponent one arrives, through blood and sweat, to the discovery of a shell that fully encloses all the deep humanity of both (Drago from machine and robot becomes man, becomes "human" as audiences begin to love Rocky's "humanity"). At the fifteenth and final round, Rocky manages to KO the mammoth opponent. Rocky's victory encourages a strong enthusiasm and the boxer, having taken the floor, pronounces the following phrases of peace in front of the Soviet authorities: a desperate cry for the concrete achievement of an idealistic peace.

«Thank you. I came here tonight and i didn't know what to expect. I seen a lot of people hating me and I didn't know what to feel about that. So I guess I didn't like you much none either. During this fight, I seen a lot of changing. The way youse felt about me and the way I felt about you. In here there were two guys killing each other, but I guess that's better than 20 million. But what I was trying to say is that if I can change, then you can change. Everybody can change!». (*Rocky IV*, 1985)

After the energetic applause of the whole audience, Rocky's thoughts go to his son:

```
ROCKY: I just want to say one thing
to my kid who should be home sleeping:
Merry Christmas, kid! I love you!
ROBERT (from home while watching TV):
I love you. (Rocky IV, 1985)
```

Rocky IV is clearly a message addressed to the leaders of the two countries so that they definitively eliminate all international tensions and move towards a reconciliation made up of shared intentions and a process of disarmament. Rocky IV is therefore the victory of nature over technology, of humanity over "non-humanity", the triumph of good over evil, of peace over war.

«TO START FROM SCRATCH»

It is 1990, the year of the fifth chapter of the saga: *Rocky V*. The direction returns to John G. Avildsen who decides to bring history back in time.

A tired and battered Rocky, after the grueling fight with Drago, returns home together with Adriana, Paulie and Tony.

During the conference in which he announces his retirement, he is angered by a wealthy boxer manager, George Washington Duke, who offers him to challenge his boxer Union Cane, but Rocky promptly refuses.

The homecoming hides an unpleasant surprise: Paulie recklessly signed papers to his accountant who scammed them, sending Rocky and his family on the street.

Due to this economic crisis, Rocky would like to accept the boxing match proposed by the rich manager, but the encounter with Drago has left serious potentially fatal brain injuries and therefore he is forced to abandon the idea of fighting on the ring.

Rocky and his family return to live in the suburbs of Philadelphia, where the son starts attending the old school (where his father also went) and becomes engaged to a girl named Jewel.

Robert, unlike his father, is not used to this street life, having led a comfortable and carefree existence up to that moment.

The son will have to face the constant teasing and bullying by some boys alone because the father's attentions are all directed to the boxer Tommy

Gunn (played by boxer Tomas David Morrison) who has chosen to train in the old gym of Mickey.

Later, there is one of the most moving scenes in the entire Rocky saga (Mickey resurfaces more powerful than ever at the vision of the old gym where it all started).

The whole scene is accompanied by Bill Conti's *Mickey* soundtrack which increases the power of the whole editing.

ROCKY: Slip the jab. Slip the jab.
MICKEY: Slip the jab, will you? Slip the jab! That's right. That's it. Hey, I didn't hear no bell!
ROCKY: Okay.
MICKEY: That's right. Slip the jab. That's it! Mentalize! See that bum in front of you. You see yourself doing right and you do right. That's pretty. That's very pretty. Time! Come here, Rock. My God, you're ready, ain't you? Apollo won't know what hit him. You're gonna roll over him like a bulldozer. An Italian bulldozer. You know, kid, I know how you feel about this fight coming up because I was young once too. And I tell you something: **if you wasn't here I probably wouldn't be alive today.** The fact that you're here and doing as well as you're doing, gives me… what do you call it? A motivization to stay alive. Because I

think that people die when they don't
want to live no more.

ROCKY: Nature's smarter than people
think.

MICKEY: **Nature is smarter than people
think. Little by little, we lose our
friends. We lose everything.** We keep
losing and losing till we say: "What
the hell am I living around here for?
I got no reason to go on". But with
you, kid… boy, **I got a reason to go
on. And I'm gonna stay alive.** And I
will watch you make good.

ROCKY: And I'll never leave you.

MICKEY: **And I'll never leave you…**
until that happens, because when I
leave you, you'll not only know how to
fight, you'll be able to take care of
yourself outside the ring, too. Okay?

ROCKY: Okay.

MICKEY: Okay. Now I got a gift for
you.

ROCKY: You didn't have to do that.

MICKEY: Wait a minute.

ROCKY: I don't need nothing.

MICKEY: Here, look at this. See that?
This here's the favourite thing that I
have on this earth. And Rocky Marciano
give me that. You know what it was?
His cufflink. And now I'm giving it to
you. And it's got to be like an angel
on your shoulder, see? And if you ever
get hurt and you feel that you're
going down, this little angel is gonna
whisper in your ear. He's gonna say:

"Get up, you son of a bitch because Mickey loves you". Okay?
ROCKY: Thanks, Mick. I love you too.
MICKEY: Jesus. Go after him, kid. Go after him.
ROCKY: Thanks. **You was the angel.**
MICKEY: There it is.
ROCKY: What happened to his other cufflink?
MICKEY: I don't know. He only give me one. He gave it to some bum.

(*Rocky V*, 1990)

The memory of Mickey is still very much alive in Rocky. In the course of our life, we come across places or emotional states that lead us back to a dear deceased person (it can happen by looking at an old photo, a video, listening to music or even a saying or something typically personal things, apparently banal, which, thanks to their simplicity, manage to make us re-emerge memories, from the most vivid to the most faded with the passage of time).

All of Rocky's trust is in Tommy Gunn who seems to be in perfect harmony with his coach, so much so that he also receives a purely personal gift, namely the socks worn by Apollo Creed for the match against Ivan Drago.

Everything seems to go well, the victories come one after the other and then Rocky returns to win in the ring as manager, until Tommy is involved by the manager Duke who convinces him to rely on him with the promise of a match against the reigning champion Cane.

On Christmas Day, Tommy shows up with his girlfriend at Rocky's house in a new and dizzying car, a gift from Duke. Rocky tries to clarify with Tommy trying to make him understand that Duke should not meddle between the two of them but the young man with all his stubbornness and presumption makes Rocky understand that he no longer even needs his help as a manager and that the next day he will sign the contract with Duke.

Rocky tries to protect him from people like Duke, as in the past Mickey did the same with him, but there is no way to make see reason.

Rocky, through his words, outlines in a decisive way how the world works.

```
ROCKY: You sign them papers, you're
like his property. You got no control.
This is a dirty business. It's full of
these thieves and gangsters. They
promise the world to every good young
fighter who comes along. They suck
them dry and leave them when they
ain't worth nothing. They leave them
in the gutter, broke. That's the way
this business is run.
```
(*Rocky V*, 1990)

The message is clear: nowadays you must always keep an eye out, traps and pitfalls are around the corner and there are always fake people who just want to take advantage of you. Rocky and his family watch the match between Tommy and Cane on TV, Rocky nonetheless cheers for Tommy, who manages to win and after the victory he thanks only and exclusively Duke (while the audience booed him and invokes the name by Rocky).

After the match Rocky and Paulie decide to go to the bar together. Tommy, not happy, wants to show everyone that he is the strongest, and he goes angry to the bar with Duke and the television organs to propose a live match against Rocky.

Here Paulie intervenes in defense of his friend by pointing out to Tommy all his ingratitude towards Rocky, so the defending champion punches Paulie by splitting his lips.

This episode makes Rocky nervous who decides to accept the match (Duke slyly pushed for a match in the ring).

«My ring's outside».

(Rocky turned to Tommy. *Rocky V*, 1990)

Challenge accepted on the only ring that Rocky knows, he manages to dominate and that will bring him once again the glory and dignity he deserves.

They both come out of the bar together with the locals and start hitting each other in the street with all the strenght.

Meanwhile, Adriana and her son also arrive who were watching all this on TV. Rocky suffers a punch in the face and falls to the ground (he begins to have visions ranging from the blows of Drago to the shouts of Adriana and the Apollo coach up to the classic encouraging words of Mickey that manage to get him back up), so he recovers and with blows he knocks Tommy down.

Once again the champion is Rocky.

Rocky believed that Tommy was his natural heir, but the truth is that he had it under his eyes.

After the battle, Rocky and his son Robert set off towards the famous Philadelphia stairways until they reach the famous statue in honor of Rocky. Here is a beautiful gesture from the father towards the son to whom he gives Mickey's twin:

«Hey, you deserve it. Thank you for being born».

(Rocky to son Robert. *Rocky V*, 1990)

This is a film that magnificently exalts paternal love and lashes out strongly against bullying, arrogance and ingratitude.

47

«GET INVOLVED»

The last chapter of the saga is *Rocky Balboa* (2006).

Rocky lives on memories, without his Adriana who visits the cemetery every morning.

He has opened a restaurant in Philadelphia called *Adrian'S* where he entertains customers by telling his personal stories in the ring.

One day on TV a computer simulation is shown that sees Rocky Balboa winning against the current heavyweight champion, Mason "The Line" Dixon (who does not enjoy much sympathy, as he does not offer spectators a show, knocking out the opponent in the first round).

Rocky, tempted by the desire to return to fight, accepts this challenge proposed by the agents of the boxer Dixon, despite having been advised against accepting this proposal by his friend Paulie and his son Robert.

So, one day, Robert goes to visit him, who tells his father that he has always lived in his shadow and with this match it will be even worse, but Rocky through these words makes his son understand that it is not at all like this.

ROCKY: You ain't gonna believe this, but you used to fit right here. I'd hold you up and say to your mother: "This kid 's gonna be the best kid in the world. This kid's gonna be somebody better than anybody every knew". And you grew up good and wonderful. It was great just watching.

Every day was like a privilege. Then the time come for you to be your own man and take on the world, and you did. But somewhere along the line, you changed. You stopped bein' you. You let people stick a finger in your face and tell you you're no good, and when things got hard, you started lookin' for somethin' to blame. Like a big shadow. I'll tell you something you already know. **The world ain't all sunshine and rainbows. It's a very mean and nasty place and I don't care how tough you are, it will beat you to your knees and keep you there permanently if you let it. You, me, or nobody is gonna hit as hard as life. But it ain't about how hard you hit. It's about how hard you can get hit and keep movin' forward. How much you can take and keep movin' forward. That's how winnin' is done!** If you know what you're worth, get what you're worth, but you gotta be willin' to take the hits and not pointin' fingers sayin' you ain't where you wanna be because of him or her or anybody! Cowards do that, and that ain't you! You're better than that! I'm always gonna love you no matter what, no matter what happens. You're my son and you're my blood. You're the best thing in my life. **But until you start believin' in yourself, you ain't gonna have a life.**

Don't forget to visit your mother.
(*Rocky Balboa*, 2006)

The next morning, in fact, Robert joins his father at the cemetery and communicates that he has abandoned his current job, expressing his desire to work with him.

The scene ends with a strong hug between the two.

Rocky undergoes specific training based mainly on strength (agility had gone away as the years go by) under the guidance of coach and friend Duke. The day of the match arrives and Rocky, according to the commentators, is doomed to defeat from the outset.

Dixon shows all his strength right from the start, already in the second round he manages to knock out the Italian stallion, who continues with all of himself until the tenth round, in which he is knocked out again.

The match seems to be over but Rocky once again finds the strength to get up, mindful of the recent speech to his son on self-esteem and his past with Adriana, managing to hit Dixon until the end of the recovery, even under the happy eyes of a woman, Marie [who, in the first chapter of the saga, when she was still a child, had received a precious teaching from Rocky and now she, an adult, single mother of a teenage son, is grateful to him and has been hired at his restaurant]. The points victory (not unanimous) goes to Dixon: the two boxers thank each other but the standing ovation is all for Rocky.

The next day he goes, as usual, with a bouquet of flowers to the cemetery to thank Adriana.

Rocky Balboa is a message to all those who believe they are not up to something.

It is the demonstration that, although life is anything but easy, there can still be strength, energy, passion and vitality in an aged body that has, for one last time, the opportunity to regain a happiness, faded with the inexorable passage of time.

LOCK UP

1989 film directed by John Flynn.

Sylvester Stallone as Frank Leone is an exemplar inmate in Northwood prison, close to release and in love with Melissa. During one night he is transferred without any reason to the Gateway maximum security prison at the behest of Drumgoole. The latter, the current prison director, is full of hatred towards Frank, due to a humiliation suffered in front of the press, inherent in an event that happened in the past in the prison that he previously managed.

Frank Leone asked permission (denied) for a free exit because he wanted to visit an old childhood friend of his hospitalized, to whom he was very attached (and thanks to his teachings, Frank was able to repair cars because the two worked together in a mechanical workshop). Frank, six months after his release, is therefore forced to suffer all sorts of physical and psychological abuse by the guards and the entire prison system.

«This is hard time, Frank. You've no rights here unless I give them to you. You feel no pleasure unless I tell you you can. This is hell».
(Drumgoole addressing Frank. *Lock Up*, 1989)

Frank manages to make friends with several inmates like him, such as Dallas (obsessed with escape plans); Eclisse (a real stand-up guy who works in the prison body shop) and Prima Base (a young boy). In the courtyard of the penitentiary,

Frank is provoked by a certain Chink Weber and one day decides to participate in a rugby match against him. The decisive point is scored by Frank, who, however, inattentive is thrown down by Weber who tears the lucky necklace given to him by his girlfriend Melissa.

Together with his friends, Frank repairs an old Ford Mustang that Eclisse was particularly fond of it. By fixing this car, everyone finds a common purpose. Frank's optimism becomes contagious for these people who think that life is now garbage and that they have nothing worth living for.

A life without any meaning.

«Nothing's dead around here until it's buried».
(Frank Leone. *Lock Up*, 1989)

Enthusiastic about what has been done, they decide to celebrate together by getting drunk:

When we're in a sober mood
We worry, work and think.
When we're in a drunken mood
We gamble, play and drink.
But when our moods are over
When your time has come to pass
We hope they bury us upside down
So the warden can kiss our ass!
("Jailhouse Poem". *Lock Up, 1989*)

First Base confides in Frank and admits that he has never done many things, including learning to drive a car. So, Frank decides to let him try, through imagination and fantasy by pushing the car with Prima Base behind the wheel.

Even if the body is imprisoned behind walls, your mind must be free to go wherever it wants.

Another request of the young boy was to hear at least once the noise of the muffler of a real car, so he starts it but instead of turning it off after a few seconds, he breaks everything and comes right into the courtyard, despite the concern and the desperation of friends.

Thus, by order of the director, the car is destroyed by Weber and other inmates, and Frank is taken to forced isolation for several days.

Frank, devastated about this experience, returns to the body shop where the environment has become terribly sad and friends stare at the destroyed Ford.

```
FRANK: It's his! This lift is his,
these tools are his, the garage is
his! The whole goddamn place is his!
And you better remember that too,
because once you start buyin' into
this… "our car", "our thing" concept,
man, you're his too!
```
(*Lock Up*, 1989)

Frank tries to make his comrades understand that all of them are just prisoners and as long as they are there they are owned by the director.

These harsh words of his are due to the fear that now afflicts him, since his release is only three weeks away and he does not want anything to happen that could affect it. The director, still dissatisfied with his revenge, orders Weber and his companions to assassinate First Base (killed in the gym, in the hope of a consequent disproportionate reaction from the hated Frank).

The latter is notified of what has happened and goes to take revenge on Weber, who, however, spares his life and takes back Melissa's lucky necklace from his neck, but he is soon after stabbed in the back.

Frank is hospitalized in the Gateway clinic, where he receives an unexpected visit from Melissa, who is soon and unfairly turned away. During the night, the protagonist receives another visit (financed by the director) from a prisoner who tells him his bad intentions: as soon as he is released from prison, he would go to rape and kill Melissa.

«Don't trust anybody».
(D.T.A. – "Word to survive by".
Frank Leone. *Lock Up*, 1989)

There is no more time. Frank, together with his friend Dallas, hatch an imminent escape plan. However, during this desperate escape, Dallas betrays Frank (in exchange for a false promise previously made with the director) who is surrounded by guards. It all turns out to be a trap: Dallas doesn't have what he wants, he just loses Frank's trust; while the latter risks remaining forever in that damned prison. However, Frank manages to free himself and save himself thanks to the help of Dallas, who sacrifices his life (his suicide/murder as redemption and final sacrifice to regain Frank's friendship).

So he decides to reach the director and take him to the electric chair to make him admit all the injustices suffered.

```
FRANK: You'll be in no time there.
I'll show you hell! (...) Dallas... he
fried, the way you're gonna fry. First
Base, took him downstairs, you broke
his goddamn neck!... I'm gonna fry
your brains. What do you know? It's a
perfect fit.
```
(*Lock Up*, 1989)

Drumgoole is then tied to the electric chair by Frank who, after the arrival of the guards and Captain Meissner, finally manages to make him confess everything.

Justice has been done. Frank finally manages to serve his sentence (two weeks) and to get out of that hell.

On the day of his release, Frank is warmly greeted by the inmates and ironically addresses Captain Meissner as follows:

```
FRANK: You know what I'm gonna miss
most about you, captain?
CAPT. MEISSNER: What's that?
FRANK: Your incredible smile.
```
(*Lock Up*, 1989)

Waiting for him outside is Melissa. The force that drove him to fight to the end.

Love that pierces injustice.

Love that survives beyond all conditions and limits. Love for life.

The desire to be free and be with this woman is the real and only driving force in Frank.

You don't get much, and what you got, you gotta protect.

(Frank Leone. *Lock Up*, 1989)

The right and honest man must have the courage to defend his innocence and to overcome injustice, to fight for truth and freedom by constantly drawing strength from love, fleeing from every prison that cages the body and soul, depriving it of the Light and filling it with fear, violence and humiliation.

RAMBO:
A MAN MARKED BY WAR

FIRST BLOOD

"Rambo has brought out a darker side of me (...) For the first time a super soldier declares war on his own country with sophisticated weapons". (Sylvester Stallone)

Stallone has managed to create a character that has now entered the collective imagination: a super soldier, a super man who is not afraid of anything or anyone.

Rambo is a simple, primordial, wild and bestial character who uses simple weapons such as a bow, a knife or an arrow, but at the same time he is a noble warrior, a demigod of Greek mythology, a hero in flesh and blood who fights against oppression and injustice.

"I like Rambo most of all. Because it seemed as if everything that the character achieved and conceived was possible (...) And the men in the audience could tell *if I was being tested, maybe I could too.* (Sylvester Stallone)

TRAUTMAN: (Addressing TEASLE) You don't seem to want to accept the fact that you're dealing with an expert in guerilla warfare. With a man who's the best. Whit guns, with knives, with his bare hands. A man who's been trained to ignore pain, ignore weather. To live off the land. To eat things that would make a billy goat puke. In

Vietnam, his job was to dispose of enemy personnel, to kill... period. Win by attrition. Well, Rambo was the best! (*First Blood*, 1982)

"To get a job done, to get it done, you'll have to blow up bridges, you'll have to look inside, do things that others may not like, you'll have to break protocols (...) Rambo's only regret is that I shouldn't have been wearing a tank top (*poor Rambo undresses to put that pathetic piece of canvas over his shoulders*) but definitely a thermal jacket. Because it was so cold. If we had to do it again, I think I would have kept the shirt. How cold it was (...) On the fourth take (in *First Blood*) I broke my ribs and spleen (...) The message was this. **If you want a job done well sometimes you have to do it yourself, whether it's popular or not**". (Sylvester Stallone)

There are five films in the Rambo series:
>*First Blood* (in Italy: *Rambo*, 1982) by Ted Kotcheff;
>*Rambo: First Blood Part II* (in Italy: *Rambo 2 - La vendetta*, 1985) by George Pan Cosmatos;
>*Rambo III* (1988) by Peter MacDonald;
>*Rambo* (in Italy: John Rambo, 2008) by Sylvester Stallone;
>*Rambo: Last Blood* (2019) by Adrian Grunberg.

"Rambo came out in October 1982: it didn't work in America, but it was successful abroad". (Mario

Kassar. Executive producer, along with Andrew G. Vajna, of *First Blood*)
"All modern action movies derive from Rambo".
(David Morrell)

The first film of the saga, based on David Morrell's 1972 novel *First Blood*, tells of a veteran in search of a normal reintegration into society who is instead pushed to violence (after going in search of a fellow soldier who discovers dead, the police and the sheriff mistreat him, triggering his reaction: Rambo puts the town to fire and sword).

In this first film, the character of John Rambo, a veteran of the Vietnam War, is a man who is very marked by this experience and is trying to reintegrate into society in some way.

Delmar Berry, the friend of unity whom Rambo visits, died of cancer due to the toxic gases [Agent Orange was a defoliant abundantly sprayed all over South Vietnam] used in Vietnam: Berry's mother tells him the tragic news and Rambo, now alone and without any friends, realizes that he is the last surviving member of the group. The soldiers who fought with Rambo in Vietnam, the members of the "Baker Squad" will be listed later by Colonel Trautman (Richard Crenna) on the radio: Messner, Ortega, Coletta, Jorgensen, Danforth, Berry and Krakauer. The horrors of war already emerge from the beginning of the film and increase, in a constant escalation, up to the moving final scene: Rambo has barricaded himself in the police station and is now surrounded.

TRAUTMAN: Think about what you're doing. The building's perimeter's covered. No exits. There's nearly 200 men out there and a lot of M16s! You did everything to make this private war happen. You have done enough damage! This mission is over, Rambo. Do you understand me? This mission is over! Look at them out there. Look at them! If you won't end this happen, they will kill you! Is that what you want? It's over, Johnny. It's over!

RAMBO: **Nothing is over! Nothing! You just don't turn it off! It wasn't my war. You asked me, I didn't ask you! And I did what I had to do to win, but someone wouldn't let us win. And I come back to the world, and I see all those maggots at the airport, protesting me, spitting. Calling me baby killer and all kinds of vile crap!** Who are they to protest me, huh? Who are they? Unless they have been me and been there, and know what the hell they're yelling about?

TRAUTMAN: It was a bad time for everyone, Rambo. It's all in the past now.

RAMBO: For you. For me, civilian life is nothing. **In the field, we had a code of honor. You watch my back, I watch yours. Back here, there's nothing!**

TRAUTMAN: You're the last of an elite group, don't end it like this.

RAMBO: Back there I could fly a gunship, I could drive a tank, I was in charge of a million dollar equipment, back here, I can't even hold a job parking cars! **Where is everybody? I had a friend, who was in the Air Force. There were all these guys, man. Back there were all these fucking guys! Who were my friends! Back here, there's nothing!** Remember Dan Forest? Wore this black headband. I took one of his magic markers, and I said: "If found, you mail this to Las Vegas", because we were always talking about Vegas, and this fucking car. This so great '58 Chevy convertible! He was talking about his car, he said we'd get cruised till the tires fell off! We were in this bar in Saigon, and this kid comes up, this kid carrying a shoe shine box. And there, he says: "Shine please, shine!". I said no, and he kept asking, yeah, and Joe would say "yeah". And I went to get a couple of beers. And the box was wired. He opened up the box, fucking blew his body all over the place. He's laying there and he's fucking screaming, there's pieces of him all over me! And I am trying to pull them off, you know… my friend! It's all over me! I got blood and everything and I am trying to hold him together, I put him together the fucking entrails keep coming out! **And nobody**

would help! He's saying, saying, "I want to go home!" Just calling my name. "I want to go home, Johnny, I want to drive my Chevy!" I said: "Why I can't find your fucking legs. I can't find your legs!". **I can't get it out of my head. It was seven years. Every day it hurts. Sometimes I wake up and don't know where I am. I don't talk to anybody. Sometimes a day. Sometimes a week.** I can't put it out of my mind. (*First Blood*, 1982)

John James Rambo was born in Arizona on July 22, 1947 (about a year after Sylvester Stallone, July 6, 1946).

Rambo's character is inspired by a true war hero, Audie Murphy (1924-1971), an American WWII veteran who received numerous honors in the United States, Belgium and France for his exploits on the battlefield.

In the various films of the saga it appears that Rambo was the son of a Navajo Indian and an Italian American woman, Marie Drago. However, in *Rambo: First Blood Part II*, Murdock (Charles Napier) states that Rambo is half Native American and half German and therefore the protagonist's origins remain uncertain.

Rambo is a highly decorated Green Beret (he was part of an elite unit of the *United States Army Special Forces* and received the *Medal of Honor*) who is found to be an outcast in his own country. Rambo is initially arrested by the arrogant sheriff, a certain

Will Teasle, from a small town named Hope, for a crime he did not actually commit but only because he is there in town to eat something.

The sheriff embodies that part of the American people who hate the losers and cannot see Rambo as a normal citizen who goes to grab a bite at a diner (he arrests him for vagrancy). He considers him a criminal and does not want to have any (human) contact with him.

The sheriff represents that America which, in order to erase that tragic page of history, does not want to have anything to do with the veterans and repudiates them, not allowing them to reintegrate into society. In Morrell's novel, Sheriff Teasle's resentment towards the protagonist is motivated by the media attention given to veterans from Vietnam, while no one had ever cared about him and the other soldiers who had fought in Korea (in the film there is only one very quick "visual" mention of Teasle's past in his office: in the frame behind him you can see the Distinguished Service Cross, the Purple Heart and the Silver Star. Even Sheriff Teasle was therefore a former war hero).

The next "manhunt" in the mountains and woods of Washington state is the epic of Rambo, a man destroyed inside, a person who has had a mental breakdown, a man lost victim of circumstances, turned into a car war from America which now refuses to recognize it as such and therefore to help it. A masterpiece from a photographic point of view (the very cold and insensitive colors, from green, to brown and gray, like "the cold" human relationship towards the veteran, are above all the materialization of the protagonist's emotional state), combined with an excellent rhythm of action scenes that keep the viewer glued to the screen and continually fascinate him.

For example, at the beginning of the film it is sunny and it seems like a beautiful day but then at the news of the death of Rambo's friend, everything appears cloudy, gray and obscured, thus carefully following the emotional and psychological aspect of the character, troubled and saddened by the tragic finding.

The environments (the forest, the crevasse, the waterfall, the cave) are highly valued both for their natural beauty and, in particular, for the exceptional deeds performed by Rambo in such contexts.

Vancouver (where the film was shot) *is very dark in the winter so it was very difficult to shoot there.*

The filmic characters are true and genuine but at the same time ambiguous: think of the police and the national guard who should be good and yet in the film they represent the antagonistic forces and prove unable to resolve the situations they face.

Their physical and mental preparation is thus ridiculed.

Rambo is therefore a hero and an anti-hero at the same time, in this paradoxical context in which the police are bad and incapable. Rambo embodies the model of the romantic hero. A rebellious and solitary man, outside society, but unlike the romantic heroes who voluntarily and with pride and proudly oppose social conventions, Rambo does not choose: it is society that forces him to follow this direction, marginalizing him.

Rambo would like a "normal" life, as Clark Kent would like. "The desire for normality", the one present now, too, in each of us.

Rambo, in the deepest inner drama, catapulted into a world unknown to him in which he is accused of "killing old and children", after having sacrificed his youth in the service of his homeland, is alone and unhappy, like the alienated and misfit Travis Bickle (Robert De Niro) in *Taxi Driver* (Martin Scorsese, 1976).

Colonel Trautman seems to be able to resolve the situation, as he embodies the more calm and reasonable part of Rambo, just like two sides of the same coin who found themselves in the same hell (that of the Vietnamese conflict), managing to survive there. But while Trautman was able to better assimilate the war experience, Rambo, like many other veterans, did not succeed at all and suffers from the so-called "post traumatic stress disorder" or "post traumatic stress disorder" (PTSD). Commanded by Deputy Sheriff Arthur Galt, the police officers carry out various brutal actions against Rambo, causing him to flashbacks of torture in Vietnam and causing him to rebel and then flee to the nearby mountains.

The subject afflicted with PTSD indeed responds with intense fear and feelings of helplessness or horror, reliving the traumatic event continuously, with persistent unpleasant and intrusive memories (from images, thoughts, or perceptions, nightmares and negative dreams, to acting or feeling as if the traumatic event was re-occurring, to the intense psychological distress and acute physiological reactivity, triggered by exposure to internal or external factors that represent some aspect of the traumatic event, towards which there is a persistent form of avoidance; difficulty falling asleep or staying asleep; irritability or outbursts of anger; difficulty concentrating; hypervigilance and exaggerated alarm responses).

"Jerry Goldsmith's music added the emotional component to the film for which it is composed. It would have softened the character. Because from the simple film he looks like a very tough character and when the music is added to the whole it becomes a wonderfully touching story".
(Sylvester Stallone)

The colonel is Rambo's only link with the world and his lifeline fixed in the "terrain of reality and humanity": Rambo only trusts him in a totally negative world, in which the hero no longer counts nothing and was totally forgotten as a person, as a human being, as a soldier who combated and fought for his nation. Indeed, he is ignored, laughed at, mistreated and hated in a country for which he was willing to do anything in war and even to die (he would have done so without any regrets, like a war machine, a robot, a dehumanized figure, precisely as required by that system and that military world, mechanized and inhuman, bestial and ruthless that created automatons to be sent to Vietnam).

The original ending of the film was changed by the will of Stallone as he considered it too pessimistic: in the alternative ending (as in Morrell's novel) Rambo freed himself from the horrors of war, clearly expressing to Trautman his will to die and the latter indulged him, killing him with a gunshot. The colonel who forged and commanded him in the conflict is the same one who frees Rambo from his demons, just as the US should do with the veterans, helping them to heal and re-integrate into society.

"RAMBO: You trained me, you made me, you kill me.

Trautman raises his gun but fails to kill this creation of his. The perfect soldier. Then Rambo pulls the trigger and shoots himself (...) It's not the kind of ending people would want to see and in the end it was decided that bringing it to life would be the best thing".

"In the book, John Rambo dies because he reaches the point of no return (...) He was so compromised by the traumatizing experiences he had in Vietnam that he became irretrievable. Irredeemable (...) I just think it shouldn't be done, it would send the wrong message. Any Vietnam veteran who sees it will think: the only solution is death. It is the only thing waiting for us at the end of the tunnel. And I don't think that's the right thing". (Sylvester Stallone)

In the final, Rambo decides to surrender and turn himself in to the police.

Trautman is Rambo's "father", his guide bearer of relevant values and meanings, his wise and encouraging teacher who embodies firmness and authority, protection and safety and Rambo at the same time is the "best son" the colonel ever had.

Rambo is not a machine, he is a helpless and unhappy child, without friends and without a future, who wanders in an unknown world and which pretends not to know him, from whom the war has taken everything away. He is a human being who needs communication and affection.

"Eventually Rambo had a nervous breakdown. And he can't handle all the repressed stimuli he's been exposed to.

And then he explodes into a madness where he can't keep his thoughts together.

And it expresses a flow of thoughts that leave it completely defenseless.

He throws himself into Colonel Trautman's arms.

And at the very end the man, the warrior becomes a child again.

And Trautman becomes a father figure.

So in the end Rambo needed love, he needed human contact". (Sylvester Stallone)

RAMBO:
FIRST BLOOD PART II

"Rambo is more self-confident, he is determined to rewrite his history". (Sylvester Stallone)

Rambo has a possibility that few have: redemption.

```
RAMBO: Mission?
TRAUTMAN: A hunt for POWs in Vietnam
(...) You interested?
RAMBO: Yeah.
```
(*Rambo: First Blood Part II*, 1985)

Jailed and forced into forced labor in a Washington penitentiary, Rambo is released by Colonel Trautman to carry out a new mission: to search for and free some US prisoners in Vietnamese military camps, but is betrayed by the corrupt American special operations commander, Marshall Murdock. whose plan was to prove that there were no more American prisoners in Vietnam, thus avoiding paying huge ransoms to the Vietnamese government, allied to the Russians.

In *Rambo: First Blood Part II*, whose direction is entrusted to G. Cosmatos who will direct Stallone also the following year in *Cobra* (1986), thanks to Reagan's militarist and patriotic policy (during the Reagan era, Rambo has changed in a political symbol of the West against the East, Freedom against Communism), the hero transforms himself into a ruthless war machine in the service of the stars and stripes nation, with the aim of recovering some forgotten fighters.

"George Pan Cosmatos (...) decided to make Rambo a more impressive character. For the first time we see him moving in his environment. It does what it was created for". (Sylvester Stallone)

The second film in the saga should have been scripted by James Cameron who had a totally different idea (*he even saw Rambo in a psychiatric hospital*) compared to Stallone and compared to what would later be the actual screenplay for the big screen.

Cameron intended to have as a starting point the film *Missing in Action* [by Joseph Zito, 1984] (in this type of low-cost film, aimed at a young and undemanding audience, with poor scripts and without great actors, who mix the characteristics of the war film and the action film, the protagonist, Chuck Norris in our specific case, who returns to Vietnam to save the missing American prisoners, manages to take a real revenge, coming to fix the most difficult situations that not even politics and diplomacy were able to solve) and above all Rambo should have been accompanied by a very over the top reporter (John Travolta), whose role would have been precisely to deepen the psychological aspect of the hero and also the personality of American prisoners.

Stallone reads Cameron's script but totally rejects this buddy movie (a type of film that has friendship as its main theme), despite later choosing a sidekick in the film (a Vietnamese girl named Co Bao, played by Julie Nickson).

Rambo, on the other hand, must be a vengeful hero, a fearless warrior who must exterminate all his enemies: this is the essence of 80s action cinema, the most effective example of cinematic "machismo" (violence, action, explosions, blows weapon).

Rambo becomes an American superman who alone manages to overcome any adversity and it is clear how the "political" role of the protagonist has changed in the course of the second film: from an outcast of society to a national hero.

Rambo: First Blood Part II, despite the various logistical problems (and related to the permissions for equipment due to the political situation), due to the heat, snakes, tarantulas and scorpions, was filmed in the jungle of Acapulco in Mexico, so that the landscape was the more varied and similar to that of Vietnam (rocks, rivers, waterfall and a paddy field created specifically for the occasion).

In the first film Rambo does not kill anyone of his own free will, both because they were policemen and inexperienced guys, and because he is a different character than *Rambo: First Blood Part II*.

RAMBO: I could have killed them all. I could have killed you. In town you're the law, out here, it's me. Don't push it! Don't push it, or I will give you a war you won't believe! Let it go. Let it go. (Rambo addressing Teasle. *First Blood*, 1982).

Rambo mutilates them but doesn't kill anyone.

Only one person dies, but only for his stupidity, taking off his seat belt on the helicopter: he is Deputy Arthur Galt. The latter, among other things, ignores the sheriff's order to capture Rambo alive and even tries to shoot him; John, however, now back to the wall and under the fire, hits the helicopter with a stone which tilts causing the fall of Galt, who smashes on the rocks below.

When Rambo sees the dead deputy sheriff crushed on a boulder, the hideous memories of all the corpses he saw in Vietnam return.

The "first" Rambo is tired of all that blood and all those deaths.

In *Rambo: First Blood Part II*, on the other hand, the protagonist, in his evolution, kills the enemies of the two armies, the Soviet one (the new opponent) and the Vietnamese one (the old one), in a context devoid of rhetoric. but imbued only with a strong sense of patriotism. In the 80s, when Vietnam becomes show and entertainment in the long series of films about American veterans, then in the current of the Vietnam movie concerning the missing soldier in action, Rambo emerges in this "stereotypical jungle", a solitary and muscular hero who leads his own personal war against Communism.

Therefore, in that period, the POW (Prisoner of war) genre was also born, dedicated to the marine taken prisoner and to be saved, with the figure of the beefy hero who sets out to rescue and recover his companions taken prisoner by the bad Communists.

Rambo seems to be able to cleverly mix various traditions of the genre: the private war of the citizen and the fantasy film like *Conan the Barbarian* (by John Milius, 1982).

The two heroes, Rambo and Conan, are the same not only for their identical muscle mass, but above all because both represent the important struggle against a system that pretends to protect us while in reality it does not take us into consideration.

The whole is often mixed with a hint of western: Rambo is a solitary avenger, skilled in the use of weapons and moves easily in the wilderness, with his face painted like the Indians.

On the other hand, the Vietnam movie has some characteristics in common with the western: both have a new border, the Far West on one side, the Far East on the other; there is a hostile landscape and primitive villains.

The Vietnam film therefore re-proposes the clash between the man of the West, bearer of the simple and positive ideals of American culture, and the immoral man of the East.

In short, in 1980 the Russians were the bad guys, the Americans the good ones.

People wanted to "win back" the Vietnam War.

The trauma of the defeat was beginning to temper, also thanks to the entry into the White House of Republican President Ronald Reagan. Vietnam was no longer a dark page that had to be quickly forgotten, but a glorious episode, albeit marked by defeat, in which American soldiers had made honor. In this panorama, the desire for revenge definitely stood out. In fact, despite having been an unjust and lost war, those who had fought it were still worthy of respect or often even heroes. Enough time had passed and it was possible to fully investigate the psychological reality of the Vietnam War. The Vietnam movie and therefore *Rambo: First Blood Part II* became the effort to rationalize, re-evaluate and exorcise the American experience in Vietnam, heavy as a boulder on the collective and individual conscience of the American community and to recover, in particular, the myth of national identity through the memory and pride of belonging to their own country.

RAMBO: (addressing TRAUTMAN) Do we get to win this time?
TRAUTMAN: This time it's up to you.
(*Rambo: First Blood Part II*, 1985)

"This phrase has been applauded by many Vietnam veterans (...) Rambo goes over there and handles the situation in his own way". (Sylvester Stallone)
Rambo always and only trusts his father figure: Colonel Trautman.
RAMBO: Murdock said he'd been with the 2nd Battalion in Kon Tum '66. The 2nd Battalion was at Kud Sank. You're the only one that I trust.
(*Rambo: First Blood Part II*, 1985)

According to Murdock, Rambo should have limited himself only to taking pictures of the prison camps (which should have been empty), but he even manages to free a prisoner. Once he arrives at the predetermined place for the meeting with the helicopter returning from the mission, Trautman notices that Rambo has freed a prisoner and communicates it to Murdock, who, however, commands the pilot to return to the base and abandon the hero to the his fate: surrounded by Vietnamese soldiers and their captains Vinh and Kinh, he is then taken to the concentration camp (where he is immersed up to his neck in pig manure, with leeches attached to his body and then tortured with electric current and burning knives by the Russian colonel Podovsky and his sergeant Yushin); Trautman, on the other hand, is forced to return to Thailand on the helicopter with a gun aimed at his head and is therefore arrested by Murdock.

Politicians were regarded as corrupt bastards. If they hadn't dealt with it, we would have won.

RAMBO: Murdock...
TRAUTMAN: He's here.
MURDOCK: Rambo, we're glad you're alive. Where are you? Give us your position, and we'll come to pick you up.
RAMBO: Murdock... I'm coming to get you! (*Rambo: First Blood Part II*, 1985)

(...) Charles Napier (Murdock) was perfect in the role of the scoundrel (...) a villain, a scumbag who cannot be trusted.

MURDOCK: What if he cracks under the pressure in that hell?
TRAUTMAN: Pressure? Rambo is the best combat Vet I've ever seen. A pure fighting machine with only a desire to win a war someone else lost. If winning means he has to die, he'll die. No fear, no regrets. And one more thing: what you call "hell", he calls home. (*Rambo: First Blood Part II*, 1985)

RAMBO: I've always believed that the mind's the best weapon. (*Rambo: First Blood Part II*, 1985)

Here is Rambo's rejection of "extreme" technology: it is man who must take responsibility for his choices.

He must not allow himself to be overwhelmed by machines: there is a strong contrast between soulless technology (its uselessness under certain conditions) and humanity, being man, the human condition with its characters, its qualities, its advantages and its limits. Humanity also understood in its relationship with nature: Rambo draws strength from it, using it to his advantage (hiding, creating weapons with what the environment offers him from time to time). "I have been training for eight months. Four hours a day. I have hardened myself. (...) Combat, archery, survival courses". (Sylvester Stallone)

(...) He woke up at five, did weight lifting and a series of exercises. After a long day of work, he went to the gym to train.

PODOVSKIJ: (Addressing Rambo, tortured with electric current) You are strong! Very strong! The strongest so far. (*Rambo: First Blood Part II*, 1985)

"Stallone requires a fast pace. He wakes up early and trains every day, without exception. And every evening (...)" (J. Nickson)

Sylvester wanted the scenes to be edited to make it appear that the arrows shot flew longer, increasing the "time of the arrow's flight".

Originality is key in action movies.

"We were always trying to invent new action scenes, all different". (Cosmatos)

The helicopters fly low, in a sort of aerial western. "(...) When in the end they are face to face, it's like a duel". (Cosmatos)

In the paradoxical and dramatic human condition, the titanic impetus in pursuit of an ephemeral bliss and happiness collides with a macabre certainty: everything is finiteness and transience.

Life's but a walking shadow, a poor player , that struts and frets his hour upon the stage and then is heard no more. It is a tale told by an idiot, full of sound and fury, signifying nothing. (*Macbeth*: act V, scene V)

Rambo's happiness really lasts a little: his constant tragedy endures in the deprivation and death of loved ones, as in the case of Co Bao.

She has lost all love to the war and despite being a warrior, she is lonely and emotionally fragile, just like Rambo.

Theirs is a love story that dies on the vine: Co Bao, after helping Rambo to escape from the prison camp, is unfortunately killed by an enemy soldier, dying in the hero's arms.

The desire to go to America and start a new life, the kiss scene, like a dream in a violent world without dreams or love, are fundamental for the character of Rambo according to Cosmatos:

"Stallone wrote this love story. It makes him more vulnerable".

CO BAO: That why they pick you? Because you like fight?

RAMBO: I am expendable.

CO BAO: What mean "expendable"?

RAMBO: It's like someone invites you to a party and you don't show up, and it doesn't really matter.

(...) CO BAO: Rambo! You not expendable. (*Rambo: First Blood Part II*, 1985)

"My character, Co Bao, only sees his fragility. She is very touched by it". (J. Nickson)

Rambo takes Co Bao's lucky charm with him and as in the first film, he goes crazy: after the girl's death, he begins his revenge, in a violence that lasts until the end of his mission.

RAMBO: (addressing MURDOCK) Mission... accomplished! You know there are more

men out there. You know where they
are. Find them, or I'll find you!
(*Rambo: First Blood Part II*, 1985)

The final scene with Colonel Trautman was shot a dozen times and each time Stallone responded with a different monologue, with different phrases and emotions, from tears to anger. Here is the definitive scene:

TRAUTMAN: What is it you want?
RAMBO: I want… what they want, and every other guy who came out here and spilt his guts and gave everything he had: for our country to love us as much as we love it. That's what I want. (*Rambo: First Blood Part II*, 1985)

"Stallone and Rambo's films have been heavily criticized, unlike Schwarzenegger or Chuck Norris. They have not criticized other actors who make violent action films, in which blood gushes out.

(…) Strange definitions of Rambo have been given. If anyone misbehaves, it's a Rambo. It is the exact opposite of what the author created. (…) The name Rambo is now in the American dictionary. For the wrong reason". (Richard Crenna)

"He is not an aggressor. He fights against the aggressors. (...) Rambo's character has become the symbol of an individual who fights against the oppressor and takes care of the situation". (Sylvester Stallone)

RAMBO III

Directed by Peter MacDonald, it is the third film in the saga and is dedicated to the "brave Afghan people".
Rambo goes to Afghanistan to free Colonel Trautman, prisoner of the Russians.

MOUSA: The Afghank King was asked to send 500 of his warriors into battle. He sent only five. His greatest five, and they won. He said "it's better to send five lions than 500 sheep". What do you think of this?
RAMBO: I think the King was lucky.
(Rambo III, 1988)

At the beginning of the film, Rambo lives in a Buddhist monastery in Thailand, helping a quiet community of monks, doing some jobs for them and sometimes having fights to raise money to donate to the monks.
GRIGGS: Well, you're sure not easy to find!
RAMBO: Why are you keepin' track?
(Rambo III, 1988)
Colonel Trautman finds Rambo to try to involve him in a new mission: to hit a Soviet commando in Afghanistan that carries out genocides against local people. However, Rambo, tired of being involved in absurd wars, refuses the invitation.

```
TRAUTMAN: You said that your war is over.
I think the one out there is, but not the
one inside you. I know the reasons you're
here, John. But it doesn't work that way.
You may try, but you can't get away from
what you really are.
RAMBO: And what is it I am?
TRAUTMAN: A full-blooded combat soldier.
RAMBO: Not any more. I don't want it.
TRAUTMAN: That's too bad, 'cause you're
stuck with it.
```
(*Rambo III*, 1988)

Rambo wants normalcy (a quiet life), like Superman, but he can't choose not to be Rambo anymore. He cannot deny his nature: it is his essence, it is his way of being and of being in the world, it is his life.

(...) Superman didn't become Superman. Superman was born Superman. When Superman wakes up in the morning, he's Superman. His alter ego is Clark Kent. His outfit with the big red "S", that's the blanket he was wrapped in as a baby when the Kents found him. Those are his clothes. What Kent wears - the glasses, the business suit - that's the costume. That's the costume Superman wears to blend in with us. Clark Kent is how Superman views us. [Bill's monologue in "Kill Bill vol. 2", Q. Tarantino, 2004].

Trautman, despite Rambo's refusal, proceeds anyway, but is attacked by enemies, captured and sent to a large mountain base to be interrogated by Russian Colonel Zaysen and Sergeant Kourov.

Griggs, the official ambassador, informs Rambo of the colonel's capture, but refuses to approve a rescue mission for fear of a possible conflict. Rambo, however, manages to obtain consent to undertake the mission, as long as he is disowned in case of capture or death.

With a huge knife, a bow with multipurpose arrows, long hair, visible muscles and a red headband, the hero is ready to go.

Rambo arrives in Peshawar (Pakistan) where he persuades arms dealer Mousa Ghani to take him to Khost, the city closest to the Russian base where Trautman is imprisoned.

```
RAMBO: I can't wait.
AFGHAN CHIEF: You must wait for help
the way we wait.
RAMBO: Then I'll go alone.
AFGHAN CHIEF: And you will die!
RAMBO: Then I'll die.
```
(*Rambo III*, 1988)

The *Mujahideen* [the fighters engaged in the *jihād* who opposed the Soviet Union in the context of the war in Afghanistan (1979-1989)], led in the town by their leader Masoud, initially did not want to help Rambo in the liberation of the colonel, even if later they arrive, on horseback, to the rescue of Trautman and Rambo himself in the final confrontation with the Soviets.

```
MOUSA: (addressing RAMBO) May God
deliver us from the venom of the
cobra, teeth of the tiger and the
vengeance of the Afghans. (Rambo III, 1988)
```
Fighting for freedom.

These valiant patriots fight for this noble and lofty ideal: to be neither slaves nor prisoners.

MOUSA: This is Afghanistan. Alexander the Great tried to conquer this country, then Genghis Khan, then the British, now Russia. But Afghan people fight hard, they never be defeated. (*Rambo III*, 1988)

Rambo, like them, also fights for freedom, but for that of his old friend, his guide, his father figure who had commanded him in Vietnam and who had helped him in the town of Hope (in the first film of the saga).

ZAYSEN: At sunrise, I will track him down, and have his skin hanging on the wall!
TRAUTMAN: You don't have to hunt him.
ZAYSEN: What?
TRAUTMAN: He'll find you.
ZAYSEN: Are you insane? One man against trained commandos? Who do you think this man is? God?
TRAUTMAN: No. God would have mercy. He won't! (*Rambo III*, 1988)

Unlike the other two films in the saga, despite the tragic nature of the war and the situations narrated, this third chapter is pervaded by a continuous humor, especially in the dialogues of questions and answers.

TRAUTMAN: You got any ideas?

RAMBO: Surrounding them, Sir.
TRAUTMAN: Helluva time for humor,
John! What do you say, John?
RAMBO: Fuck 'em! (*Rambo III*, 1988)

MOUSA: What is this for?
RAMBO: It's blue light.
MOUSA: What does it do?
RAMBO: It turns blue. (*Rambo III*, 1988)

MOUSA: God must love crazy people!
RAMBO: Why?
MOUSA: He makes so many of them!
(*Rambo III*, 1988)

MOUSA: You're sure you don't want to
stay? You fight good for a tourist!
(*Rambo III*, 1988)

In *Rambo III*, Rambo is truly extraordinary, a super man who endures pain beyond all limits: while in the first film he healed his wounds himself (without anesthesia), here, wounded by a bullet, he even cauterized the hole on his flesh afterwards extracting the bullet, sprinkling it with gunpowder and setting it on fire.

In the final scene, driving a tank, Rambo collides with the Russian colonel Zaysen, driving a helicopter, face-to-face at full speed and shooting themselves just before impact: a terrible frontal collision destroys the helicopter and Zaysen dies, while Rambo survives.

ZAYSEN: Who are you?

RAMBO: Your worst nightmare. (*Rambo III*, 1988)

Rambo then gives his lucky charm received in turn by Co Bao to the Afghan boy, an orphan named Hamid who helped him in the mission. Rambo born to a father (and mother) from whom he was separated in his youth due to the (Vietnam) war, created and educated by another "father" (Colonel Trautman), never had and will never have a son. Like a "Frankenstein", generated by America and the needs of the conflict, the protagonist, "alive but not alive", "dead inside", is not given the opportunity to give his life.

This gift of Rambo's lucky charm to the Afghan boy could therefore symbolize the "gift of life" of a mother (Co Bao, the only woman with whom the protagonist has had a love affair, albeit very short, in the entire saga) that passes from the hands of the "father" (Rambo) to the "son" (Hamid).

Rambo, Co Bao and Hamid are alone, without any affection and their destinies have been deeply marked by the war.

The family that the hero never had is ideally realized in this gesture.

At the end of the battle, Rambo and Trautman bid farewell to the *Mujahideen* and leave Afghanistan.

RAMBO

In the penultimate film of the saga, three films and two decades later (2008), John Rambo has retired to northern Thailand, where he works as a snake-hunter on a boat along the Salween River, bordering Burma. In the Asian state there is a terrible and "silent" civil conflict, which has lasted for more than seventy years since 1949, between the Burmese military regime and the local Karen ethnic group.

Having abandoned their weapons for a long time, Rambo meets a group of Protestant missionaries in search of the "American river guide": Sarah Miller (Julie Benz) and Michael Burnett explain to him that the Burmese military has filled the streets with mines and so they beg him to lead them across the Salween River to their destination in order to bring supplies of medicines, food and bibles to the population. After initially refusing to go as far as Burma, Rambo agrees to accompany them.

BURNETT: We compensate you for a few hours of your time that will help change people's lives.

RAMBO: Are you bringing in any weapons?

BURNETT: Of course not.

RAMBO: You' re not changing anything.

BURNETT: It's thinking like that, that keeps the world the way it is!

RAMBO: Fuck the world. (*Rambo*, 2008)

Rambo in the "solitude of Oedipus in Colonus", even more atrocious than the Greek one (in the Sophoclean tragedy, Oedipus the vagabond goes to Colonus, enjoying however the company of his daughter Antigone), has now become an *Übermensch*.

According to Rambo, the world is evil and will never change: there are only war and hatred that must be answered exclusively with fierce and brutal violence.

Religion and love cannot change anything.

Rambo "overman or Nietzschean superman" looks straight into the eyes of Medusa (a Greek mythological figure, one of the three Gorgons, the only mortal among them, whose power was to petrify anyone who met their gaze), not looking away from snakes; he says yes to life and accepts it in its tragic dimension, with the bloody knife of the most precious and divine blood, beyond all illusions and lies that man relies on to flee from the desert and the abysses, not accepting hardness of life.

Rambo, on the other hand, crosses them, overpass them, plunges into the darkest and most terrible depths and re-emerges with force, bearing the darkest and obscurest night, the Sun that has moved away and the earth that sinks lower and lower under his feet, accepting the tragicity of existence.

Rambo is faithful to blood and to the earth (the home of the man who generated him and to whom he will return), he is the child who says yes to life, creating and shaping it and he is ready to face death at any time it takes him. He grabs the head of the snake that is entering his throat, bites it and takes its head off: he has transformed into a human god who has gone beyond human (in some scenes where he works metal, Rambo remembers Hephaestus, god Greek of fire, forges, engineering, sculpture and metallurgy, with immense strength in his arms and shoulders). In *Rambo*, drama and tragedy take over and materialize in unprecedented violence: more and more blood, more and more deaths (in *First Blood* only one dead, in *Rambo: First Blood Part II* 69, in *Rambo III* 132 and here well 236, with an average of 2.59 deaths per minute and with the first death after only three minutes and four seconds).

Not only physical violence but also internal violence, with torments, nightmares, past demons that return and surface in Rambo's suffering mind.

Colonel Trautman is now dead [the film was in fact dedicated to actor Richard Crenna (who passed away in 2003), present here in *Rambo* only through archive images]: Rambo, without his guide, his mentor, is more alone that never.

He is the most silent [and then violent] Rambo that has ever been seen up to that moment: he speaks very little and inspires fear only with his eyes, in a land devastated by war, whose people are suffering like him. The protagonist's silence reflects this "silent" conflict (of which the media is silent), "the invisible" and unknown Burmese genocide.

Rambo has lost faith in people.

The only one he cares about (and wants to talk to) is Sarah. Only for her he will agree to accompany the group of missionaries with his boat.

SARAH (addressing RAMBO): Maybe...
Maybe you've lost your faith in
people, but you must still be faithful
to something. You must still care
about something. Maybe we can't change
what it is, but trying to save a life
isn't wasting your life (...)
RAMBO: Sarah, because of you, we're
going upriver. Anytime you want to
turn around, it's done.
SARAH: Ok. (*Rambo*, 2008)

The meeting on the river and the consequent killing of the pirates by Rambo is the first sign of the subsequent violence that Sarah and her group will face: after having led them to the pre-established place, a poor Burmese village full of war mutilated, missionaries suffer an assault by government troops, witnessing the slaughter of women and children. Four missionaries, including Sarah, are taken hostages by the cruel Commander Pa Tee Tint. On a dark and rainy night, Rambo has flashbacks in a dream:

Company leader calling Raven.
Come on, Raven.
What am I?
You made me this way.
A full-blooded combat soldier.
You just don't turn it off.
Talk to me, Johnny.
You just don't turn it off!
It's over!

Nothing is over!
When are you gonna come full circle?
I know the reasons you're here, John.
No!
Aren't you curious to see how things might have changed back home?
You've done enough damage.
You're always gonna be tearing away at yourself until you come to terms with what you are.
Until you come full circle. (Here is the theme of the eternal recurrence of the *Übermensch*)
So you're just gonna stay here forever?
John!
I wanna go home!

The nightmare is interrupted by Pastor Arthur Marsh who tells him (two weeks after the event) that the missionaries have been imprisoned and taken to a Burmese military camp, commanded by Tint. Marsh has also hired a group of mercenaries, led by a certain Lewis, with the aim of bringing the missionaries home: Rambo agrees to lead the mercenaries up the river to the war zone.

Only Sarah, with her will and determination, with her love for life and Trautman (in a dream) managed to shake Rambo "the man", cold and imperturbable (almost no longer human) and awakened Rambo "the warrior" from the illusory torpor.

This is Rambo's curse: he doesn't want to fight anymore but he is forced to.

Live for nothing or die for something.

(John Rambo. *Rambo*, 2008)

Something good that is worth fighting for again.
Fighting for Sarah.
Having a goal in life is of fundamental importance.

Don't waste your life. Don't let your existence go by against nature. Accept your own destiny.

You know what you are? What you're made of? War is in your blood. Don't fight it. You didn't kill for your country. You killed for yourself. The gods are never gonna make that go away. When you're pushed... killing's as easy as breathing.

(John Rambo. *Rambo*, 2008)

Rambo, together with the mercenaries, manages to free the missionaries from the prison camp.

The fugitives arrived on the boat that should lead them to safety, however, are joined by Burmese soldiers. In the final scene, Rambo exterminates the entire Burmese army with a powerful machine gun and kills the commander (who, among the many crimes committed, was also guilty of pedophilia) with a machete. Finally, tired of the fighting, the hero decides to permanently return home to

Arizona, to his father's farm. "Rambo is extremely easy to understand, he's not a complicated guy.

For him what is right is right and what is wrong is wrong. The bad should be punished and the weak protected.

And I think this ties in with the stories we grew up with and the legends are based on (...)

I didn't want it to be about a crime, drugs, or jewelry theft.

I wanted it to talk about humanity (...) **Burma** [(...) it is a huge responsibility to try to tell the story of the Karen (...) a splendidly brutal experience].

(…) About Julie Benz [*Sarah Miller in the movie*].

I needed a person who emanated this kind of optimism and credibility (...)

This is the simplest, most primitive and truest film that can be found.

The scope of the film is very broad because those are humble people in a wasteland, vast and hostile.

I think the symbolism of nature is overwhelming and **Rambo feels that those people are devastated, left on their own. So we see that devastated world into which he will descend. And in this journey into darkness there is a sense of hope and spectacle, in the sense that the man can overcome the sense of despair and by trying to save Sarah and the missionaries, he is also saving a part of himself"**. (Sylvester Stallone)

RAMBO: LAST BLOOD

Fifth and final chapter of the saga, directed by Adrian Grunberg (2019), *Rambo: Last Blood* is in direct continuity with *First Blood*.

[David Morrell, who wanted to make a film that would tell the narrative arc of the protagonist in an intimate way, had to detach himself from this last chapter, whose screenplay was built by Sylvester Stallone and Matthew Cirulnick].

However, *Rambo: Last Blood* undoubtedly recovers, at least in the first part of the film, the more intimate and personal dimension of First Blood, but not strictly connected to political or social issues, as in the case of the first film of the saga.

In *Last Blood*, John Rambo fragile, melancholy and thoughtful, forced to acknowledge having led a life troubled by the loneliness and affection of a few, a "civilized" and silent man who moves slowly and is at ease only with animals, coexists "shamefully" with his true nature as a warrior who has sown death all his life and who is almost waiting for the right opportunity to emerge and take over the "civilized" man. So the screenplay divides everything into two segments, albeit with a strong imbalance due to the re-emergence of Rambo's violent and deadly nature, which after a slow start accelerates almost brutally in the second part of the film.

Now old (without the classic appearance, with long hair and headband: a Rambo for the first time with short hair), wounded in the soul and still suffering from post-traumatic stress disorder (due to which he takes medicine), the protagonist is nevertheless always ready to protect the people he loves and to fight against the evil ones in an unjust world to which, both victim and executioner, he has always felt he did not belong.

Rambo seems to have found an "apparent" period of peace, having lived for ten years in Arizona (on the farm where he spent his childhood), in the loving warmth of a true adoptive family with the elderly Maria (Adriana Barranza) and her niece Gabrielle (Yvette Monreal).

The girl, orphaned of her mother and abandoned by her father, represents for "uncle John" (as Rambo is affectionately called by her) the daughter she never had.

In Rambo who has forever abandoned the idea of a love life, despite his monsters never ceasing to smolder, Gabrielle symbolizes the only example of purity in a negative world, her only affection in an existence cursed by the solitude.

The ghosts return from the hero's past: the specters of comrades who died in battle decades before, who never left the old fighter, those of a life made of mistakes, of dead ideals and buried in the jungle, together with the enormous sense of the survivor's fault towards the friends he had to bury. The dark cry of pain, the desperate strength of a symbol of a vanished America, John Rambo is the emblem of failure, of the Reaganian epic trampled by history, by the economic crisis and by the changes of a society that never ceases to hide his hatred for the insane and marginalized.

An inexorable mistake leads Gabrielle to cross alone the border into Mexico: the girl, after revealing to Rambo that a friend of hers (Gizelle) has tracked down her biological father (Miguel) in Mexico, goes there in secret, against the want of Rambo and Maria, to know the reasons why the father abandoned her in the past.

Gizelle takes Gabrielle to Miguel's home, where he reveals that he never really cared about her and her mother.

Heartbroken Gabrielle goes with her friend to a local club, where she is drugged and kidnapped by sponsors of a Mexican cartel.

And *Last Blood* becomes the last, epic rescue mission in a violent and dark territory, Mexico, the victim of ruthless bosses of a cartel specialized in human trafficking, the brothers Victor and Hugo Martinez (Oscar Janeada and Sergio Peris-Mecheta).

Rambo is transformed here into an authentic westener hero: in the dilated and rarefied atmospheres of the prairie, pain and revenge inexorably affect the hero of Vietnam, who crosses the border with Mexico, starting his own new and modern private war (the American citizen doing justice for himself). Western, action, war and gangster movies are mixed in a film in which the character of Rambo stands out constantly and only, always invincible and always alone against the horror of the world.

He arrived in Mexico, he questions both Miguel and Gizelle, who leads him at the club where Gabrielle was last seen and then he confronts El Flaco, the man who last spoke to the girl.

However, the hero is beaten by the men of the Martinez brothers (many against one).

A journalist named Carmen, in search of justice for the murder of her sister at the hands of Hugo's gang, treats Rambo and reveals that she has investigated the Martinez brothers.

Rambo then breaks into one of the brothels, killing several men until he finds Gabrielle on drugs, who unfortunately dies of an overdose in the hero's pickup truck before he can get her home. The anger at death and the disfigurement of the girl's beauty and purity are also reflected in the wrinkled and "leathery" face of Rambo, increasingly ugly and "monstrous". Rambo, beside himself, sends Maria away and sets numerous traps in the underground tunnels and on the ranch, in anticipation of a future confrontation.

The protagonist then breaks into Victor's home, killing him along with several guards.

Thirsty for revenge, his brother Hugo leads a group of hit men to Rambo's farm, where they all die, with clearly exposed, gory and almost hyper-realistic wounds and mutilations, sparing the spectator in nothing.

Rambo employs the same guerrilla tactics that were used against him in Vietnam many years earlier: as the Mexican gang attacks his ranch, Rambo manages to surprise his enemies, causing them to explode and immediately return underground, disappearing completely before the survivors even have the opportunity to react. Inside the caves, he kills his opponents with handmade traps, including a pit at the bottom of which spears sprout, alluding to the snare used against the Americans in Vietnam.

After all, Rambo, like the Vietnamese during the conflict, is inferior in number and military power, but he is defending his home and knows his land better than the enemy.

Saving Hugo last, Rambo literally rips his heart out, in one of the bloodiest final confrontations of the entire saga.

After the battle, Rambo, tired and wounded, sits on the porch of his father's house, vowing to keep fighting and keep alive the memory of his loved ones.

RAMBO: **I've lived in a world of death. I tried to come home, but I never really arrived.** A part of my mind and soul got lost along the way, but my heart was still here where I was born, where I would defend to the end the only family I've ever known, the only home I've ever known. **All the ones I've loved are now ghosts. But I will fight to keep their memory alive forever.** (*Rambo: Last Blood*, 2019)

The credits feature a stunning montage of the iconic character in all five films in the series. The final images show Rambo, like a western hero, once again riding a horse and appearing to be heading, not towards sunset, but towards a nearby mountain.

Rambo reflects me a lot: as a young man he was all muscles and lonely but over the years he had the need to start a family (...) In this way I showed the human side of Rambo [almost a dramatic comedy] (...) We Italians are tenacious and very passionate. - Sylvester Stallone - He was born on July 6, 1946 at a charity in Hell's Kitchen, near Manhattan; the parents are Jacqueline Labsofish and Frank Stallone (son of Italian immigrants: Silvestro Stallone and Pulcheria Nicastri, originally from Gioia del Colle, in the province of Bari, and emigrated to the USA in the 1930s).

"One of the worst diseases that affects humanity is loneliness (...) **even Rambo can no longer be alone.**

He really needs human contact, needs love (...)

What is common to all generations are our emotions, our hearts (...) **if you can write a story that touches the heart, your audience will never abandon you** (...)". (Sylvester Stallone)

Rambo teaches us to take the side of the weakest, the poor, the oppressed and to fight against injustice.

Rambo fought for his country in Vietnam but also alongside the Afghan people and the Karen ethnic group in Burma, for the American veterans prisoners, for Trautman, for Sarah, for Gabrielle. He fought for himself and against himself.

Rambo teaches us to fight for freedom and for our homeland, for our family and for the people we love.
He teaches us to resist pain, both physical and moral, emotional or psychological, since he, unjustly losing all recognition, witnessing the denial of his own merits, was offended and insulted, tortured mentally and physically.
But above all he teaches us to live with the past and with death.
Rambo has lost everything.
Everything. Every person he loved. They are all dead.
Rambo teaches us to bear the loss of loved ones and to accept death as the very essence of life.
He teaches us to never lose the memory of loved ones, to continue fighting and living.

OVER THE TOP

« SOME FIGHT FOR GLORY... HE BATTLES FOR THE LOVE OF HIS SON»

1987 film directed by Menahem Golan.

Lincoln Hawk (Sylvester Stallone) is a lonely truck driver who tries to regain the trust of his son, after the separation from his wife because of the rich and hated father-in-law who through his money has overwhelmed him and permanently estranged him from his family.
By the will of his wife, dying of a terminal illness and not yet operated, who has never stopped loving Lincoln, he obtains the authorization to personally pick up his son Mike from the military school where he studies. He reluctantly decides to leave with his father and then go to visit his mother at the hospital.
Thus begins a journey of several days, which at first is full of mistrust and resentment on the part of Mike towards his father, described by his grandfather as an unreliable and of little value. As time goes by together, things begin to change, Mike attends his father's impromptu arm wrestling match in a fast-food restaurant. The bond between the two strengthens more and more with the passage of time (Lincoln manages to use those few hours to teach his son everything he knows and can, from morning training to driving on the truck to the real specialty: arm wrestling).
In an arcade, an arm wrestling match, wanted by Lincoln, between his son Mike and some arrogant boys takes place. In the first round, despite the encouragement of his father, Mike is defeated, so out of anger and bitter disappointment he runs out

of the arcade, but here he receives a precious lesson of life.

LINCOLN: Now you lost back there because you beat yourself. You let yourself get beat. I know you can do it. You're a special kid. You're my boy, do you understand? But you're also a spoiled rich brat who's always had everything done for him. It's time to do it for yourself, and you can do it. **The world meets nobody halfway.** Do you understand that? **If you want it,** Mike, **you gotta take it.** Do you hear me? Go in there and try. I know you can win. But even if you don't, so what? So you lose. As long as you lose like a winner, it doesn't matter. 'Cause you did it with dignity. If you don't go in there, you're gonna be sorry. You'll regret it your whole life, you know what I mean? Go on. I know you can do it. (*Over The Top*, 1987)

In life we always have challenges to face, we have to fight until we win. If we don't succeed, that's okay, at least we tried until the end, because there is no greater remorse than that of not having at least tried. Mike manages to win and is delighted. He calls his mother to find out how she is and tell her everything he is doing with his father. Then, Lincoln talks to his wife, but, just outside the telephone station, Mike is kidnapped by criminals by order of his father-in-law. Lincoln, after a violent chase, manages to recover his son: the bond between the two is strengthened even more.

Everything seems to be going well until they go to the hospital where they learn that their mother died in the operating room in the morning. In desperation, Mike accuses his father of the time lost with him and of not having had the opportunity to see his mother still alive because of him, so he takes a taxi and returns to live with his grandfather.

After the funeral celebration, Lincoln, now alone again, decides to go directly to his father-in-law's luxurious home to recover Mike. Here, he is prevented from accessing and so he enters by force, carrying everything forward with his truck. He manages to enter the villa and see his son on the stairs, but the security men immobilize him.

Denounced and imprisoned, the protagonist has an interview with the secretary of the rich father-in-law who points out his bad economic situation and the large sum that he will have to pay back.

Lincoln has only one way to get out of there: leave the state and never see his son again.

His son is also present at the interview, and asks him directly what he should do: Mike refuses to go and live with him, despite the sad situation, Lincoln manages to teach him another life lesson.

LINCOLN: Mike, I want you to remember something. The world meets nobody halfway, remember that. You gotta do what's best for you. Always do that.

(*Over The Top*, 1987)

«The world meets nobody halfway».

Meanwhile, Mike returns home and begins to turn everything upside down in search of the letters, which his father admitted to having sent many times, until he can find them (it was his grandfather who hid them). Lincoln, on the other hand, sells the only thing he has left: his truck (while retaining its symbol, a steel hawk).

He manages to scrape together some money that will all bet on himself as a winner at the World Armwrestling Championship in Las Vegas, in which he will take part (WINNING Lincoln Hawk is quoted 20 to 1).

Now, Mike fully believes in his father and aware of his participation in the tournament, among a thousand pitfalls he manages to get to Las Vegas.

His father-in-law, desperate to have Mike with him and get rid of Lincoln for good, offers him a large sum of money (a check for five hundred thousand dollars), but he promptly refuses.

I got a family. When this is over, I'm coming to get him. (Lincoln Hawk. *Over The Top*, 1987)

Money can never buy true love.

Lincoln will be able to triumph in the final against the giant Bob "Bull" Hurley (five times world champion in arm wrestling). The bet on which he has staked everything turns out to be a winning one: he can leave with his new truck and have an economic security from which to start over. This time no longer alone, under the scorching sun of the long crossings of the United States of America, but together with the only person he fought for to the end: his son Mike.

Lincoln's victory is the definitive conquest of his son's love, obtained through a spirit of sacrifice and for having believed in himself to the end, ignoring the opinion of others.

If you want something you have to fight.

In life, what matters is to always walk tall, have self-confidence and never give up. Never.

The value of a man is not based on the material goods he possesses but on the love he has to offer.

Overcome any limit, any obstacle or barrier.

Face any enemy and any difficulty.

Start from scratch.

Fight.
Continue to live
And never give up.

Antonio Raimondi
Rocco Raimondi

AUDIOVISUAL SOURCES

All interviews, quotes and dialogues have been partially extracted from the following sources.

Rocky (USA, 1976. Director: John G. Avildsen. Production Co: Chartoff-Winkler Productions).

Rocky II (USA, 1979. Director: Sylvester Stallone. Production Co: Chartoff-Winkler Productions).

Rocky III (USA, 1982. Director: Sylvester Stallone. Production Co: Chartoff-Winkler Productions, United Artists).

Rocky IV (USA, 1985. Director: Sylvester Stallone. Production Co: United Artists, Chartoff-Winkler Productions).

Rocky V (USA, 1990. Director: John G. Avildesn. Production Co: United Artists, Chartoff-Winkler Productions, Star Partners III Ltd.).

Rocky Balboa (USA, 2006. Director: Sylvester Stallone. Production Co: Metro-Goldwyn-Mayer, Columbia Pictures, Revolution Studios, Chartoff-Winkler Productions, United Artists).

First Blood (Rambo) (USA, 1982. Director: Ted Kotcheff. Production Co: Anabis N.V., Cinema'84, Elcajo Productions).

Rambo: First Blood Part II (USA, 1985. Director: George Pan Cosmatos. Production Co: Estudios Churubusco Azteca S.A., Anabasis N.V.).

Rambo III (USA, 1988. Director: Peter MacDonald. Production Co: Carolco Pictures).

Rambo (USA, 2008. Director: Sylvester Stallone. Production Co: Lionsgate, The Weinstein Company, Millenium Films, Equity Pictures Mediefonds GmbH & Co. KG IV, EFO Films, Rogue Marble).

Rambo: Last Blood (USA, 2019. Director: Adrian Grunberg. Production Co: Lionsgate, Millennium Films, Campbell Grobman Films, Dadi Film Group, Balboa Productions, Templeton Media, Nu Boyana Film Studios, Tenerife Film Commission, Santa Cruz Media, Visit Portugal, Picture Portugal, Film i Väst, Filmgate Films, Davis-Films).

Over The Top (USA, 1987. Director: Menahem Golan. Productions Co: Cannon Group, Golan-Globus Productions, Warner Bros.).

Lock Up (USA, 1989. Director: John Flynn. Productions Co: White Eagle, Carolco Pictures, Gordon Company).

Biography (Sylvester Stallone), Documentary from History Channel. (IMDb movie data, *https://www.imdb.com/* for more details)

Special Contests from DvD: Rambo (Collector'S Edition, Distributed in Italy by Eagle Pictures SpA, 2017).

Special Contests from DvD: Rambo 2 La Vendetta (Collector'S Edition, Distributed in Italy by Eagle Pictures SpA, 2017).

Special Contests from Dvd: John Rambo (Collector'S Edition, Uncensored Version, 2010, Distributed in Italy by Mondo Home Entertainment S.p.A.).

Sylvester Stallone Interview Rambo: Last Blood (Collider Interviews, YouTube Channel)

Rambo Last Blood: Behind the Scenes (backstage of Rambo:Last Blood, extract from YouTube)

Sylvester Stallone, The Making of Lock Up (1989, special contests from YouTube)

This work, purely for didactic and illustrative use, does not intend to violate in any way the copyright laws relating to the extracts of the films and interviews contained therein, as well as specifically cited and recognized in this publication. All rights are reserved to the legitimate owners.

On the cover: Sylvester Stallone (Author: Anastasiya Fedorenko, Description: Русский: Сильвестр Сталоне) Image also usable for commercial purposes, freely modified with a platinum monochrome effect.

In: *commons.wikimedia.org/wiki/File:Сильвестр_Сталоне._Фото_Анастасии_Федоренко.jpg*

As Italian authors, we have done everything possible to ensure that the content of the original work reaches you unaltered in its translation. We apologize for any lexical and morphological errors in the English language. Thanks for your understanding.

For any information or other requests you can contact the authors at: **raimondibrothers@gmail.com.**

Thank you.

Printed in Great Britain
by Amazon